50 Grain and Greens Recipes for Home

By: Kelly Johnson

Table of Contents

- Quinoa with Spinach and Poached Egg
- Millet Porridge with Kale
- Buckwheat Pancakes with Blueberries
- Oatmeal with Chia Seeds and Spinach
- Amaranth Frittata with Broccoli
- Barley Salad with Brussels Sprouts
- Farro Salad with Lemon Vinaigrette
- Brown Rice Salad with Avocado
- Quinoa Tabbouleh with Mint
- Spelt Salad with Grilled Asparagus
- Lentil Soup with Swiss Chard
- Quinoa Vegetable Soup
- Barley and Mushroom Soup
- Millet and Carrot Soup
- Farro and Kale Soup
- Stuffed Peppers with Brown Rice
- Quinoa and Black Bean Burgers
- Farro Risotto with Peas
- Buckwheat Noodles with Bok Choy
- Millet-Stuffed Acorn Squash
- Roasted Sweet Potatoes with Quinoa
- Sautéed Kale with Brown Rice
- Garlic and Herb Farro
- Spinach and Feta Quinoa Cakes
- Grilled Corn with Amaranth
- Savory Oatmeal Cookies with Spinach
- Quinoa Energy Bites with Nuts
- Rice Cakes with Avocado
- Millet Crackers with Hummus
- Kale Chips with Nutritional Yeast
- Quinoa Pudding with Coconut Milk
- Brown Rice Pudding with Raisins
- Amaranth Cookies with Dark Chocolate
- Buckwheat Brownies
- Oatmeal Chocolate Chip Cookies

- Spinach and Banana Quinoa Smoothie
- Kale and Almond Milk Smoothie
- Berry and Oat Smoothie
- Green Protein Smoothie with Chia
- Avocado and Spinach Smoothie
- Grain Bowl with Roasted Vegetables
- Mediterranean Grain Bowl with Hummus
- Buddha Bowl with Brown Rice
- Quinoa and Roasted Beet Bowl
- Farro Bowl with Grilled Chicken
- Herb-Infused Quinoa
- Spicy Lentils with Greens
- Sautéed Garlic Greens with Grain
- Savory Grain Stuffing
- Spelt and Vegetable Stir-Fry

Quinoa with Spinach and Poached Egg

Ingredients:
1 cup cooked quinoa
2 cups fresh spinach
2 eggs
1 tbsp olive oil
Salt and pepper to taste

Instructions:
In a skillet, heat olive oil and sauté spinach until wilted. In a separate pot, poach eggs. Combine quinoa and spinach, season with salt and pepper, and top with poached eggs.

Millet Porridge with Kale

Ingredients:
1 cup millet
3 cups vegetable broth
2 cups chopped kale
1 tbsp olive oil
Salt and pepper to taste
Instructions:
Cook millet in vegetable broth until tender. In a separate pan, sauté kale in olive oil until softened. Stir kale into millet, season, and serve warm.

Buckwheat Pancakes with Blueberries

Ingredients:
1 cup buckwheat flour
1 tbsp sugar
1 tsp baking powder
1/2 tsp baking soda
1/4 tsp salt
1 cup milk
1 large egg
1/2 cup blueberries

Instructions:
In a bowl, whisk buckwheat flour, sugar, baking powder, baking soda, and salt. In another bowl, mix milk and egg. Combine wet and dry ingredients, fold in blueberries, and cook on a skillet until golden.

Oatmeal with Chia Seeds and Spinach

Ingredients:
1 cup rolled oats
2 cups water or milk
1 cup fresh spinach
2 tbsp chia seeds
Salt to taste
Instructions:
Cook oats in water or milk until creamy. Stir in chia seeds and spinach until wilted. Season with salt and serve warm.

Amaranth Frittata with Broccoli

Ingredients:
1 cup cooked amaranth
4 large eggs
1 cup steamed broccoli
Salt and pepper to taste
1 tbsp olive oil

Instructions:
In a bowl, whisk eggs with salt and pepper. Stir in amaranth and broccoli. Heat olive oil in a skillet, pour in the mixture, and cook until set. Finish under the broiler if desired.

Barley Salad with Brussels Sprouts

Ingredients:
1 cup cooked barley
1 cup Brussels sprouts, thinly sliced
1/4 cup olive oil
2 tbsp lemon juice
Salt and pepper to taste

Instructions:
In a large bowl, combine cooked barley and Brussels sprouts. Whisk together olive oil, lemon juice, salt, and pepper, and toss with the salad.

Farro Salad with Lemon Vinaigrette

Ingredients:
1 cup cooked farro
1/2 cup cherry tomatoes, halved
1/4 cup cucumber, diced
1/4 cup feta cheese, crumbled
2 tbsp olive oil
1 tbsp lemon juice
Salt and pepper to taste

Instructions:
In a bowl, combine farro, tomatoes, cucumber, and feta. Whisk together olive oil, lemon juice, salt, and pepper, then pour over salad and toss gently.

Brown Rice Salad with Avocado

Ingredients:
1 cup cooked brown rice
1 avocado, diced
1/2 cup black beans, rinsed
1/4 cup red onion, diced
2 tbsp lime juice
Salt and pepper to taste

Instructions:
In a bowl, combine brown rice, avocado, black beans, and red onion. Drizzle with lime juice, season with salt and pepper, and mix gently.

Enjoy these nutritious recipes!

Quinoa Tabbouleh with Mint

Ingredients:
1 cup cooked quinoa
1 cup parsley, chopped
1/2 cup mint, chopped
1 cup cherry tomatoes, diced
1/4 cup olive oil
Juice of 1 lemon
Salt and pepper to taste

Instructions:
In a bowl, combine quinoa, parsley, mint, tomatoes, olive oil, lemon juice, salt, and pepper. Toss well and serve chilled.

Spelt Salad with Grilled Asparagus

Ingredients:
1 cup cooked spelt
1 bunch asparagus, grilled
1/4 cup cherry tomatoes, halved
1/4 cup feta cheese, crumbled
2 tbsp balsamic vinegar
1 tbsp olive oil
Salt and pepper to taste

Instructions:
In a large bowl, combine spelt, grilled asparagus, tomatoes, and feta. Drizzle with balsamic vinegar and olive oil, then season and toss gently.

Lentil Soup with Swiss Chard

Ingredients:
1 cup lentils, rinsed
4 cups vegetable broth
2 cups Swiss chard, chopped
1 onion, diced
2 carrots, diced
2 cloves garlic, minced
1 tsp cumin
Salt and pepper to taste

Instructions:
In a pot, sauté onion, carrots, and garlic until softened. Add lentils, broth, cumin, salt, and pepper. Simmer until lentils are tender, then stir in Swiss chard and cook until wilted.

Quinoa Vegetable Soup

Ingredients:
1 cup quinoa, rinsed
4 cups vegetable broth
1 cup carrots, diced
1 cup celery, diced
1 cup zucchini, diced
1 can diced tomatoes
1 tsp thyme
Salt and pepper to taste

Instructions:
In a pot, combine all ingredients and bring to a boil. Reduce heat and simmer until quinoa and vegetables are tender. Adjust seasoning as needed.

Barley and Mushroom Soup

Ingredients:
1 cup barley, rinsed
4 cups vegetable broth
1 cup mushrooms, sliced
1 onion, diced
2 carrots, diced
1 tsp thyme
Salt and pepper to taste

Instructions:
In a pot, sauté onion and carrots until soft. Add mushrooms and cook until browned. Stir in barley, broth, thyme, salt, and pepper. Simmer until barley is tender.

Millet and Carrot Soup

Ingredients:
1 cup millet, rinsed
4 cups vegetable broth
2 cups carrots, chopped
1 onion, diced
2 cloves garlic, minced
1 tsp ginger, grated
Salt and pepper to taste

Instructions:
In a pot, sauté onion, garlic, and ginger until fragrant. Add carrots, millet, broth, salt, and pepper. Simmer until millet and carrots are tender.

Farro and Kale Soup

Ingredients:
1 cup farro, rinsed
4 cups vegetable broth
2 cups kale, chopped
1 onion, diced
2 cloves garlic, minced
1 tsp thyme
Salt and pepper to taste

Instructions:
In a pot, sauté onion and garlic until soft. Add farro, broth, thyme, salt, and pepper. Simmer until farro is tender, then stir in kale and cook until wilted.

Stuffed Peppers with Brown Rice

Ingredients:
4 bell peppers, halved
1 cup cooked brown rice
1 cup black beans, rinsed
1 cup corn
1 tsp cumin
1 cup salsa
Salt and pepper to taste

Instructions:
Preheat oven to 375°F (190°C). In a bowl, combine rice, beans, corn, cumin, salsa, salt, and pepper. Stuff mixture into pepper halves. Place in a baking dish, cover with foil, and bake for 30 minutes.

Enjoy these wholesome recipes!

Quinoa and Black Bean Burgers

Ingredients:
1 cup cooked quinoa
1 can black beans, rinsed and drained
1/2 cup breadcrumbs
1/4 cup onion, finely chopped
1 tsp cumin
1/2 tsp chili powder
Salt and pepper to taste
Olive oil for cooking

Instructions:
In a bowl, mash black beans and mix with quinoa, breadcrumbs, onion, cumin, chili powder, salt, and pepper. Form into patties. Heat olive oil in a skillet and cook burgers until golden on both sides.

Farro Risotto with Peas

Ingredients:
1 cup farro
4 cups vegetable broth
1 cup peas (fresh or frozen)
1 onion, diced
2 cloves garlic, minced
1/2 cup Parmesan cheese (optional)
Salt and pepper to taste
Olive oil for sautéing

Instructions:
In a pot, sauté onion and garlic in olive oil until soft. Add farro and cook for 1-2 minutes. Gradually add broth, stirring frequently, until farro is tender. Stir in peas and cheese, season, and serve.

Buckwheat Noodles with Bok Choy

Ingredients:
8 oz buckwheat noodles
2 cups bok choy, chopped
2 tbsp soy sauce
1 tbsp sesame oil
1 clove garlic, minced
1 tsp ginger, grated
Sesame seeds for garnish

Instructions:
Cook buckwheat noodles according to package instructions. In a skillet, heat sesame oil and sauté garlic and ginger. Add bok choy and cook until wilted. Toss noodles with bok choy and soy sauce, then garnish with sesame seeds.

Millet-Stuffed Acorn Squash

Ingredients:
2 acorn squashes, halved and seeded
1 cup cooked millet
1/2 cup cranberries
1/4 cup walnuts, chopped
1 tsp cinnamon
Salt and pepper to taste

Instructions:
Preheat oven to 400°F (200°C). Mix millet, cranberries, walnuts, cinnamon, salt, and pepper. Fill acorn squash halves with the mixture and place in a baking dish. Add water to the dish and bake for 30-35 minutes until squashes are tender.

Roasted Sweet Potatoes with Quinoa

Ingredients:
2 sweet potatoes, diced
1 cup cooked quinoa
2 tbsp olive oil
1 tsp paprika
Salt and pepper to taste

Instructions:
Preheat oven to 425°F (220°C). Toss sweet potatoes with olive oil, paprika, salt, and pepper. Roast for 25-30 minutes until tender. Combine with quinoa and serve warm.

Sautéed Kale with Brown Rice

Ingredients:
2 cups kale, chopped
1 cup cooked brown rice
2 tbsp olive oil
2 cloves garlic, minced
Salt and pepper to taste

Instructions:
In a skillet, heat olive oil and sauté garlic until fragrant. Add kale and cook until wilted. Stir in brown rice, season with salt and pepper, and heat through.

Garlic and Herb Farro

Ingredients:
1 cup farro
2 cups vegetable broth
2 cloves garlic, minced
1 tbsp fresh parsley, chopped
1 tbsp fresh thyme, chopped
Salt and pepper to taste

Instructions:
Cook farro in vegetable broth according to package instructions. In a pan, sauté garlic until fragrant. Combine cooked farro with garlic, parsley, thyme, salt, and pepper.

Spinach and Feta Quinoa Cakes

Ingredients:
1 cup cooked quinoa
2 cups fresh spinach, chopped
1/2 cup feta cheese, crumbled
1/2 cup breadcrumbs
1 egg
Salt and pepper to taste
Olive oil for cooking

Instructions:
In a bowl, mix quinoa, spinach, feta, breadcrumbs, egg, salt, and pepper. Form into patties. Heat olive oil in a skillet and cook cakes until golden on both sides.

Enjoy these delicious and nutritious recipes!

Grilled Corn with Amaranth

Ingredients:
4 ears of corn, husked
1 cup cooked amaranth
2 tbsp olive oil
Salt and pepper to taste
Fresh herbs (optional)

Instructions:
Preheat grill to medium heat. Grill corn until charred, about 10 minutes. In a bowl, mix cooked amaranth with olive oil, salt, and pepper. Serve grilled corn topped with amaranth and fresh herbs if desired.

Savory Oatmeal Cookies with Spinach

Ingredients:
1 cup rolled oats
1/2 cup whole wheat flour
1/2 cup spinach, finely chopped
1/4 cup olive oil
1/4 cup grated cheese (optional)
1 egg
1/2 tsp baking powder
Salt and pepper to taste

Instructions:
Preheat oven to 350°F (175°C). In a bowl, combine oats, flour, spinach, olive oil, cheese, egg, baking powder, salt, and pepper. Drop spoonfuls onto a baking sheet and bake for 15-20 minutes until golden.

Quinoa Energy Bites with Nuts

Ingredients:
1 cup cooked quinoa
1/2 cup nut butter
1/4 cup honey or maple syrup
1/2 cup mixed nuts, chopped
1/4 cup dark chocolate chips (optional)
1/2 cup oats

Instructions:
In a bowl, mix all ingredients until well combined. Roll into small balls and refrigerate for at least 30 minutes before serving.

Rice Cakes with Avocado

Ingredients:
4 rice cakes
1 ripe avocado
1 tbsp lime juice
Salt and pepper to taste
Optional toppings: sliced radishes, cherry tomatoes, or herbs
Instructions:
Mash avocado with lime juice, salt, and pepper. Spread the mixture onto rice cakes and top with optional toppings as desired.

Millet Crackers with Hummus

Ingredients:
1 cup millet flour
1/4 cup olive oil
1/4 cup water
1/2 tsp salt
Hummus for serving

Instructions:
Preheat oven to 350°F (175°C). In a bowl, combine millet flour, olive oil, water, and salt. Roll out the dough and cut into desired shapes. Bake for 15-20 minutes until crisp. Serve with hummus.

Kale Chips with Nutritional Yeast

Ingredients:
1 bunch kale, washed and torn into pieces
1 tbsp olive oil
1/4 cup nutritional yeast
Salt to taste

Instructions:
Preheat oven to 350°F (175°C). Toss kale with olive oil, nutritional yeast, and salt. Spread on a baking sheet and bake for 10-15 minutes until crispy.

Quinoa Pudding with Coconut Milk

Ingredients:
1 cup cooked quinoa
1 can coconut milk
1/4 cup honey or maple syrup
1 tsp vanilla extract
Cinnamon for sprinkling

Instructions:
In a saucepan, combine quinoa, coconut milk, honey, and vanilla. Cook over medium heat until warmed through. Serve warm, sprinkled with cinnamon.

Brown Rice Pudding with Raisins

Ingredients:
1 cup cooked brown rice
2 cups milk (dairy or plant-based)
1/4 cup raisins
1/4 cup sugar (or to taste)
1 tsp vanilla extract
Cinnamon for sprinkling

Instructions:
In a saucepan, combine brown rice, milk, raisins, sugar, and vanilla. Cook over medium heat until thick and creamy. Serve warm, sprinkled with cinnamon.

Enjoy these tasty and healthy recipes!

Amaranth Cookies with Dark Chocolate

Ingredients:
1 cup amaranth flour
1/2 cup butter or coconut oil, softened
1/2 cup brown sugar
1/4 cup honey or maple syrup
1 egg
1/2 tsp vanilla extract
1/2 tsp baking soda
1/4 tsp salt
1/2 cup dark chocolate chips

Instructions:
Preheat oven to 350°F (175°C). In a bowl, cream together butter and brown sugar. Beat in egg and vanilla. In another bowl, whisk amaranth flour, baking soda, and salt. Combine wet and dry ingredients, then fold in chocolate chips. Drop spoonfuls onto a baking sheet and bake for 10-12 minutes.

Buckwheat Brownies

Ingredients:
1 cup buckwheat flour
1/2 cup cocoa powder
1/2 cup sugar
1/4 cup melted coconut oil
1/2 cup milk (dairy or plant-based)
1 tsp vanilla extract
1/2 tsp baking powder
1/4 tsp salt

Instructions:
Preheat oven to 350°F (175°C). In a bowl, mix buckwheat flour, cocoa powder, sugar, baking powder, and salt. In another bowl, combine melted coconut oil, milk, and vanilla. Mix wet and dry ingredients, then pour into a greased baking dish. Bake for 20-25 minutes.

Oatmeal Chocolate Chip Cookies

Ingredients:
1 cup rolled oats
1/2 cup all-purpose flour
1/2 cup butter or coconut oil, softened
1/2 cup brown sugar
1/4 cup granulated sugar
1 egg
1 tsp vanilla extract
1/2 tsp baking soda
1/4 tsp salt
1/2 cup chocolate chips

Instructions:
Preheat oven to 350°F (175°C). In a bowl, cream together butter and sugars. Beat in egg and vanilla. In another bowl, combine oats, flour, baking soda, and salt. Mix wet and dry ingredients, then fold in chocolate chips. Drop spoonfuls onto a baking sheet and bake for 10-12 minutes.

Spinach and Banana Quinoa Smoothie

Ingredients:
1 cup cooked quinoa
1 banana
1 cup fresh spinach
1 cup almond milk (or milk of choice)
1 tbsp honey or maple syrup (optional)
Instructions:
In a blender, combine all ingredients and blend until smooth. Adjust sweetness if needed and serve chilled.

Kale and Almond Milk Smoothie

Ingredients:
1 cup kale, stems removed
1 banana
1 cup almond milk
1 tbsp almond butter
1 tsp honey (optional)

Instructions:
Blend all ingredients until smooth. Adjust sweetness and consistency as desired, then serve.

Berry and Oat Smoothie

Ingredients:
1 cup mixed berries (fresh or frozen)
1/2 cup rolled oats
1 cup yogurt or milk (dairy or plant-based)
1 tbsp honey or maple syrup (optional)
Instructions:
Blend all ingredients until smooth. Adjust sweetness if desired and enjoy chilled.

Green Protein Smoothie with Chia

Ingredients:
1 cup spinach or kale
1 banana
1 cup almond milk
1 tbsp chia seeds
1 scoop protein powder (optional)
Instructions:
Blend all ingredients until smooth. Serve immediately for a refreshing boost.

Avocado and Spinach Smoothie

Ingredients:
1 ripe avocado
1 cup spinach
1 cup almond milk
1 tbsp lime juice
1 tbsp honey (optional)

Instructions:
Blend all ingredients until creamy and smooth. Adjust sweetness if needed and serve chilled.

Enjoy these delicious and nutritious recipes!

Grain Bowl with Roasted Vegetables

Ingredients:
1 cup cooked grains (quinoa, farro, or brown rice)
2 cups mixed vegetables (bell peppers, zucchini, carrots)
2 tbsp olive oil
Salt and pepper to taste
Fresh herbs for garnish
Instructions:
Preheat oven to 400°F (200°C). Toss vegetables with olive oil, salt, and pepper, then roast for 20-25 minutes. Serve over cooked grains, garnished with fresh herbs.

Mediterranean Grain Bowl with Hummus

Ingredients:
1 cup cooked grains (quinoa or farro)
1/2 cup cherry tomatoes, halved
1/2 cucumber, diced
1/4 cup olives, sliced
1/4 cup hummus
1 tbsp olive oil
Salt and pepper to taste

Instructions:
In a bowl, combine cooked grains, tomatoes, cucumber, olives, and olive oil. Season with salt and pepper, then top with hummus before serving.

Buddha Bowl with Brown Rice

Ingredients:
1 cup cooked brown rice
1 cup steamed broccoli
1/2 avocado, sliced
1/2 cup chickpeas, rinsed
1 tbsp tahini
Lemon juice to taste

Instructions:
In a bowl, layer brown rice, broccoli, avocado, and chickpeas. Drizzle with tahini and lemon juice before serving.

Quinoa and Roasted Beet Bowl

Ingredients:
1 cup cooked quinoa
1 cup roasted beets, diced
1/2 cup goat cheese (optional)
1/4 cup walnuts, chopped
2 tbsp balsamic vinaigrette

Instructions:
Combine quinoa and roasted beets in a bowl. Top with goat cheese, walnuts, and drizzle with balsamic vinaigrette before serving.

Farro Bowl with Grilled Chicken

Ingredients:
1 cup cooked farro
1 grilled chicken breast, sliced
1 cup arugula
1/2 cup cherry tomatoes, halved
1 tbsp olive oil
Salt and pepper to taste

Instructions:
In a bowl, layer farro, grilled chicken, arugula, and tomatoes. Drizzle with olive oil and season with salt and pepper before serving.

Herb-Infused Quinoa

Ingredients:
1 cup cooked quinoa
1/4 cup parsley, chopped
1/4 cup basil, chopped
1 tbsp olive oil
Salt and pepper to taste
Instructions:
In a bowl, mix cooked quinoa with herbs, olive oil, salt, and pepper. Serve as a side or base for other dishes.

Spicy Lentils with Greens

Ingredients:
1 cup cooked lentils
2 cups kale or spinach, chopped
1 tsp chili powder
1 tbsp olive oil
Salt to taste

Instructions:
In a pan, heat olive oil and sauté greens until wilted. Add cooked lentils, chili powder, and salt. Stir until heated through and serve.

Sautéed Garlic Greens with Grain

Ingredients:
2 cups greens (kale, spinach, or Swiss chard)
1 cup cooked grains (quinoa or brown rice)
2 cloves garlic, minced
1 tbsp olive oil
Salt and pepper to taste
Instructions:
In a skillet, heat olive oil and sauté garlic until fragrant. Add greens and cook until wilted. Serve over cooked grains, seasoned with salt and pepper.

Enjoy these wholesome and satisfying grain bowls!

Savory Grain Stuffing

Ingredients:
4 cups cooked grains (such as quinoa, farro, or brown rice)
1 onion, diced
2 celery stalks, diced
2 carrots, diced
2 cloves garlic, minced
1 tsp dried thyme
1 tsp dried sage
1/2 cup vegetable broth
Salt and pepper to taste
Fresh parsley for garnish

Instructions:

1. Preheat oven to 350°F (175°C).
2. In a skillet, sauté onion, celery, and carrots in a little olive oil until softened, about 5-7 minutes. Add garlic and cook for another minute.
3. In a large bowl, combine the sautéed vegetables, cooked grains, thyme, sage, salt, and pepper.
4. Pour in the vegetable broth and mix until well combined.
5. Transfer to a greased baking dish and bake for 20-25 minutes until heated through. Garnish with fresh parsley before serving.

Spelt and Vegetable Stir-Fry

Ingredients:
1 cup cooked spelt
2 cups mixed vegetables (bell peppers, broccoli, carrots)
2 cloves garlic, minced
1 tbsp soy sauce
1 tbsp sesame oil
1 tsp grated ginger
Salt and pepper to taste
Sesame seeds for garnish

Instructions:

1. In a large skillet or wok, heat sesame oil over medium-high heat.
2. Add garlic and ginger, sautéing for about 30 seconds until fragrant.
3. Add mixed vegetables and stir-fry for 5-7 minutes until tender-crisp.
4. Stir in the cooked spelt and soy sauce, mixing well. Cook for an additional 2-3 minutes to heat through.
5. Season with salt and pepper, and garnish with sesame seeds before serving.

Enjoy these delicious and hearty dishes!